# The 5 Firsts

## A Simple System to On-board, Engage, and Retain Top Talent

- The first hour
- The end of the first day
- The end of the first week
- The presentation of the first paycheck
- The end of the first 30 days

Mel**Kleiman**

Humetrics Holdings, Inc.
222 Lombardy Dr., Sugar Land, Texas 77478
(713) 771-4401
*http://www.humetrics.com*
*http://www.kleimanhr.com*

Library of Congress Catalog Card Number
2010902202
ISBN 978-1-893214-06-4

**Our deepest thanks to all the great clients we've worked with over the past two years to develop, implement, and improve this system.**

## Also by Mel Kleiman, CSP

Hire Tough, Manage Easy –
How to Find and Hire the Best Hourly Employees

267 Hire Tough Proven Interview Questions
for Hiring the Best Hourly Employees

100 + 1 Top Tips, Tools & Techniques
to Attract & Recruit Top Talent

Recruit Smarter, Not Harder

So. You Got the Job, Now What?

180 Ways to Build a Magnetic Culture

# The 5 Firsts:
# How to Improve Productivity
# and Profits in Five Easy Steps

Let's face it, when it comes time to face the daunting prospect of starting a new job, most of us feel like little kids again, but in grownup bodies. That's why kindergarten teachers are trained to be sensitive to what's on every kid's mind the first day of school:

- What's the teacher like and will she like me?
- Will I have friends here?
- How hard is the work?
- How will I be graded?
- What if I have to go to the bathroom?

And every new person you hire wonders the grownup version of the very same things. Unfortunately, few employee orientation and training programs answer these basic questions and even fewer make new hires feel welcomed as valuable new members of the team. In fact, the contrary is more often true.

**Case in Point...**

Several years ago, my firm conducted an employee turnover study for a Midwestern convenience store chain and contacted approximately 1,000 former (mostly hourly) employees who had left in the previous year.

When asked if they would consider a return to the company, about 20 percent said they would and the majority of those were the people who had recently left. Most of the 20 percent were in their first or second week of starting a new job.

As most everyone in the workforce has experienced firsthand, the first few weeks in a new job are usually confusing, overwhelming, and stressful. Who wouldn't wish they could have their old job back?

This is why we have developed and fine-tuned *The 5 Firsts* – a simple, straightforward employee on-boarding and retention program that can help any organization keep new hires engaged, productive and happy – as well as improve the bottom line.[1]

Its design took into account the results of a long-term research study which concludes the most profitable business organizations in North America share three things in common: (1) the lowest employee turnover in their respective industries, (2) their employees are highly engaged and (3) they aggressively promote women to executive positions.[2]

In order to build on the correlation between lower turn-over, higher profits, and the relationship skills women bring to the workplace, *The 5 Firsts* consists of five simple steps designed to create a personal, emotional connection between the employee, the job, and the company that reduces turnover and improves profits.

---

[1] If you'd like to learn how to attract quality applicants and select the ones who will be the best on the job, read my earlier book, *Hire Tough, Manage Easy*, because effective employee recruiting and selection are the foundation of the employee retention program detailed here.

[2] Research conducted by Roy. D. Adler, PhD, Pepperdine University annually since 1990.

Every time I discuss the importance of the first impressions employers make on new hires, many meeting participants are anxious to volunteer stories of their own nightmarish first days on a job they soon left – or later wished they had left sooner. You'll find several of these scary *New Job Hell* stories throughout these pages.

**The tragedy of all *New Job Hell* stories is that the only people who get frustrated and turned off by an unprofessional, disorganized, boring, haphazard, first day or week on the job are the ones who are energetic, enthusiastic and who want to be productive as soon as possible.**

**Few hiring managers seem to realize there is a direct link between the impression they make on the employee during the new hire's first few days on the job and subsequent employee turnover.**

New hires report for duty excited, nervous, anxious, and eager to please. What happens during the course of the first day will determine whether he or she leaves excited, happy, and proud, or disappointed, confused, and frustrated. And you can bet that even before that new employee gets home from work, a friend or family member will ask, *So, how'd it go? Do you like it? How's your boss? Do you like the people you work with?*

That's why the first two steps of ***The 5 Firsts*** help ensure no matter what transpires during that first day, the new hire's answer is: *Great! I love it. The people are super and I can't wait to go back tomorrow.*

The way things stand now, about 50 percent of new, hourly employees quit in the first six months and most of those leave during the first month. And then there are those who mentally quit during the first week, but stay around a lot longer. These folks often get the impression that either they and/or what they do are not important, so they never become fully productive. (These are the more than 70 percent of the American workers polled by Gallup who describe themselves as either not engaged or totally unengaged[3] with their jobs.) Then there are those who feel it would look bad to leave too soon or who want to put off the pain of looking for a new job, so they just mark time for six months or a year and then leave you in the lurch.

**How much pain do you feel when you realize you have to fire someone? Ask yourself how much pain you have to create to cause a new employee to leave. No one likes to look for a job; no one takes a job planning to quit; no manager wants to look for a new employee. So, what do you suppose happens between the time the applicant eagerly accepts the position and the day that person quits?**

---

[3] Uninterested, bored, going through the motions while watching the clock.

To put it bluntly, the employer blows it.

After spending all the time and money it took to recruit and select a new hire, consider the many ways employers destroy any potential return-on-people-investment:

- The new hire wasn't able to work the first day because there was no uniform (no desk, no computer, no phone, no trainer, etc.).
- The first two days were spent in an orientation devoted to filling out forms, reading policy manuals, safety drills, rules and regulations.
- The new hire was thrown in without any orientation or training at all and told by either actions or words to "sink or swim."
- The hiring manager did not tell the new hire the full range of his or her duties and responsibilities and/or about the unpleasant tasks required.
- The hiring manager made promises about opportunities for advancement and raises that could not be kept.

Other common misrepresentations include a failure to tell applicants about more or fewer work hours than stated and when and how raises and promotions are awarded.

When the hiring manager glosses over the tough parts of the job and reality doesn't match what the new hire expects, there's bound to be another costly breakup.

**When employers make these kinds of mistakes, how long do you think it takes for new hires to feel they're in the wrong place?[4]**

And what a waste. Wasted time and money recruiting. Wasted time and money screening and interviewing. Wasted time and money training.

And what a shame. Especially when, once the right person is hired, there are five simple steps anyone can take to ensure the new hire's experiences reinforce their decision to join the team.

*The 5 Firsts* program is designed to help you efficiently establish a positive, lasting relationship with every new hire and is keyed to these important events:
1. The first hour
2. The end of the first day
3. The end of the first week
4. The first paycheck
5. The end of the first 30 days

To learn how to leverage the power of first impressions, minimize costly employee turnover, and maximize profitability, read on…

---

[4] While our main focus here is hourly employees, this kind of first impression disconnect happens at every level --- all the way up to the boardroom. *The 5 Firsts* suggested herein can easily be adapted to protect your organization's investment in exempt and non-exempt employees alike.

## Scary Story #1:

# Hired Today, Gone Tomorrow

One HR professional told me about her daughter's experience. Heather was a 16 year old honor student with no prior work experience. She was hired by a nationwide quick-serve restaurant chain to work part-time after school three days a week, all day Saturdays, and to help out some Sundays. The hiring manager scheduled Heather to show up for training on a Saturday morning at 10:00.

Heather arrived on time, but her manager was tied up in a meeting, so, the assistant manager took over and got her started on the required paperwork. By the time she finished filling out forms, it was getting busy, so the assistant manager said: *Let's get you on the line so you can help out. Here, Jill can show you the ropes.*

Jill had been there all of four weeks and had never trained anyone before. To make matters worse, Jill confided to Heather she was looking for a new job. *Heather*, she said, *you may be new, but you'll find out right away how the manager will tell you one thing and the assistant manager will tell you another. I can't wait to get out of here.* The rest of day was just as chaotic and the manager never did find time to meet with his new hire.

Heather went home frustrated and confused. When she told her mom about it, her mom said: *If you don't like it, you don't have to go back. You can certainly find another job as easily as you got this one.*

Heather called and told the manager she would not be back because "the work was too hard." (At the end of the call, I can easily imagine the clueless manager hung up and muttered something like: *These kids today just don't have any work ethic.*)

Heather found a job at another restaurant two days later and her first day was great. Her manager took her around and introduced her to everyone and spent some time telling her about the company and how important her job was. He checked back with her frequently during her first week to see how it was going. When he presented her first paycheck, he complimented her on what a great team player she was and told her to keep up the good work.

Heather stayed on until she finished high school. When in college, she returned and helped out at Christmas and during the summers. In her last year of college, she was the assistant manager in charge of training new hires.

# The 1st First: The First Hour

*First impressions are lasting.*

The first hour on the job is the most important time you will ever spend with your new employee. There will never be another time when that person will be as receptive, willing to listen, and wanting to understand your expectations as well as to live up to them. This meeting will set the tone for the entire relationship the new hire will have with you and the organization, so it pays to get it right.

To maximize your long-term, return-on-people investment, use the first hour on the job to leverage the power of first impressions.[5] When you invest this time up front, you get to enjoy the rewards of lower turnover and greater employee engagement later.

The following suggestions outline how you could best spend the first hour so, no matter what else may happen during the course of the day or even the first couple of days (boring paperwork, confusion over training processes, etc.), the new hire will still be happy and excited to have joined your team (instead of bored to tears from

---

[5] Make this first hour meeting standard procedure whenever someone is promoted or transferred into your department as well.

filling out forms in a stuffy room while hearing about policies and procedures all day or, worse, being thrown into chaos without enough training).

## First Hour Guidelines

Your goal is to ensure every new employee walks away from that first hour with a positive impression.

1. **They need to feel "chosen" (not just hired) to be a valued member of the team.**

2. **They need to understand how important their job is and how it fits into the big picture.**

3. **They need to feel they've made the right decision and leave the meeting proud to be part of your organization.**

**If your organization puts new hires through a great orientation and training program before they actually "report for duty," your job becomes easier, but the first hour meeting is no less important.**

**If that orientation and training program is anything less than great, the first hour meeting is vital. It's your opportunity to correct a poor first impression, rekindle the new hire's excitement and enthusiasm, develop a positive relationship, and set expectations.**

### Before this first meeting:

1. Select the new hire's start date and time so it does not coincide with your normal start time, overlap shift changes, or any other busy or chaotic time. You might ask the new hire to arrive 45 minutes before the normal start time or whenever things are quieter and more orderly. The goal is to be able to

give your new person your undivided attention for the first 45 minutes to one hour.

2.   Be ready for the new employee. Nothing makes a new hire feel less important than when an employer is not prepared for their arrival. Your failure to prepare tells a new hire you are disorganized, have poor planning skills, and you don't think the job or the new person matter much.

3.   Check to be sure the people who conduct the training/orientation program are able to provide all the tools, materials, and information the new hire needs to feel comfortable and that the first day:

- Includes the opportunity for the new hire to do something productive and receive positive reinforcement for doing it (or something else) well.
- Focuses in part on what's in it for the employee rather than 100 percent on what the company wants/needs.
- Does not have long, dull, boring stretches. (The mind can only absorb as much as the seat will endure.)
- Does not put them in any situation that has the potential to make them feel stupid.

4.   Put the shoe on the other foot and ask yourself what you would like to have happen during your first hour on a new job and how would you like to be treated and make it part of your program.

5.   Review this person's employment application and your interview notes. Look for schools, interests, hobbies, activities this person may have in com-

mon with you and other team members as ice-breakers. Make sure you have gathered all the necessary materials (employee handbook, uniform, badge, etc.) and the meeting space is clean and comfortable.

6. Assign a buddy or mentor to be a "go to" person for the new employee for the first few weeks. Ask the mentor to invite the new hire to join him/her on breaks for the first few days.

## Meeting Agenda:

1. **Meet & Greet:** Be on time; greet your new person warmly and restate your name and title. Let others know in the new hire's presence you're not to be disturbed; offer a snack and/or beverage and make small talk (weather, traffic, sports, current events) until you can see the new hire has relaxed.

2. **Share Information & Set the Stage:** Tell the new hire a little about yourself, especially how you came to work for the company and how you got to your present position. To reinforce their decision to accept the job, tell them why you like your job and the company. Then discuss your general expectations – how you want them to communicate with you and about your management style.

   My practice is to tell all new employees it is not my job to manage them, it is their job to manage me. I let them know I expect them to make decisions and not come to me looking for work to do or "permission" to do the right thing. I encourage them to ask me when they're not sure about something the first time, but, after that, to operate as independently as possible. Some managers may prefer an employee stick strictly to the job description and get management approval for anything else. The important thing is to give the new hire the information he/she needs to successfully work with you.

3. **Correct Poor First Impressions:** If the new hire has been or will go through a separate training and/or orientation session, ask for this person's feedback on that program afterwards and, if appropriate, suggestions as to how it might be improved. Congratulate him or her on making it through and reinforce their decision to take the job once again.

4. **Determine Motivators:** In order to effectively manage, motivate, and reward your new employee down the road, take this time to find out what his/her drivers are using some of the suggested questions that follow. Be sure to make it a conversation though – not an inquisition. (While you may have covered some of this ground in the interview, a job applicant has a totally different mindset than a new hire and you're more likely to get the unvarnished truth now.)[6]

   - *I just want you to know we're glad you've joined our team and we look forward to working with you. So, tell me, why did you decide to take this job?*

---

[6] The examples are only suggestions. You are encouraged to expand on these by also covering expectations and responsibilities unique to you and/or your organization. Put the scripted suggestions into your own words. You should also modify them to fit each particular new hire. For instance, you may not spend as much time with an experienced 52 year old as you would with a teen embarking on his or her first work experience.

- *Looking back on your past experience at school or work, what motivates you to do your very best? What discourages you from doing your best?*
- *When someone does an outstanding job, how do you think they should be rewarded?*
- *I've noticed some people learn best by being carefully walked through a new task step-by-step while others would rather jump right in and try it with very little instruction. So, tell me, how do you learn best?*

5. **Set Expectations:** *"You know we had a lot of other applicants for this job. Tell me, why do you think we hired you over everyone else?* [Listen to their response, then...] *Let me tell you why we hired you...* (list person's positive traits) *and because your job here is very important; if it weren't important we would not have hired anyone to do it. In fact, your job is more important than mine in many respects because if I make a mistake or don't do something on time, not a single one of our customers will probably ever know about it. On the other hand, what we'll count on you to do impacts every customer and whether or not they continue to do business with us. So, if your job ever seems unimportant to you in any way, please remember customer service is what we care about most around here and your job is all about customer service.*

Talk about how their job fits into the big picture of not only your location or department, but companywide as well and then...

*As your manager, let me tell you what's most important to me…"* (list the traits you value most in the person who does this particular job --- strict adherence to corporate values, customer service, teamwork, honesty, reliability, etc.).

Follow this with a discussion of your organization's values, mission, objectives, community service activities, etc.

Then spell out your preferred way for employees to handle conflicts, questions, etc. *Should you ever have any work-related issues of any kind arise, I want you to…*

6. **Theft Prevention:** Employee theft is still the #1 cause of shrink in North America. Many employees see the coffers fill with cash each day, but do not understand how thin margins really are. Devise a simple example or take a few minutes to explain how much of every dollar in sales is actually profit. (For example, you could create a drawing of a dollar bill with different sections representative of the different major expense categories and one for profits.)

7. **Reassurance & Agenda:** *"You will learn lots of new things today, but please don't feel you have to remember it all. That would be impossible for anyone. It's normal to feel pretty overwhelmed at the end of the first few days. And we want you to know we don't expect you to be perfect. We're all human and make mistakes from time to time and sometimes that's the best way to learn. So feel free to ask questions and if I'm not*

*available or not around, you can ask* [person's name] *and he/she can probably help.*

Outline how the rest of the day will be spent and with whom. Recommended activities include:

- Facilities tour (point out restrooms, location and use of time clock, safety equipment, first aid kits, exits, break areas, etc.)

- Introductions to friend/mentor and the rest of the staff (can be made at the same time as the tour)

- Necessary paperwork

- Orientation (review job description, organization chart, benefits, work rules, employee handbook/manual, performance appraisals, etc.)

- Training (including health and safety rules and regulations)

8. **Questions:** *What questions do you have for me? Is there anything you're wondering about or that is unclear?*

9. **Closing:** *During your first few weeks, I want to encourage you to let me know if you think there's a better way to do your job. You'll experience it with "fresh eyes" and you may see things we've haven't. We're always looking for ways to improve things for our customers and our employees, so please let me know. Once again, we're glad to have you here. I'll find you at the end of the day today to see how it went and I'll also check with you at the end of your*

*first week. If I get tied up somehow and you don't see me before the end of the day today or at the end of your first week, I want you to find me because it's that important. And, if you have any questions or concerns that your (trainer/ mentor/buddy) can't answer, I want you to be sure to get with me about that too. Now let me take you to....*

This may seem like a lot to cover, but, with use, will become second nature. Use the First Day Checklist in the Appendix to keep these meetings on track.[7]

---

[7] For a complimentary, full size copy of the checklist, visit *www.Humetrics.com*, Knowledge Center, Forms & Tools.

**Scary Story #2:**

# And Then There Were Two

*Here's another great story a phone center technical support person shared. While he managed to get through the first day on the job successfully, the rest of the people in his group of new hires didn't fare so well.*

*My current job had a pretty epic first day. After the first three weeks in training, I show up 30 minutes late and all my supervisor says to me is: "Thank God, I thought you bailed." I then spent the rest of the day in queue with no down time between calls while a lot of people from my training class ended up quitting (two people just up and walked out), getting sent home, needing a supervisor to bail them out, or sitting with another rep while they got their bearings. One of the people that walked out was a previous Apple tech. The only other person besides me that didn't flake out to some extent was someone who'd worked tech support for Dell.*

*Nothing quite like knowing you're one of the better people in your training class.*[8]

---

[8] Or realizing how dismally poor the training program was.

# The 2<sup>nd</sup> First:
# The End of the First Day

*What a difference a day makes, only eight little hours...*

As we've said before, new hires report for duty excited, nervous, anxious, and eager to please. What happens during the first day will determine whether he or she leaves excited, proud, and happy or disappointed, confused, and frustrated. And you can bet when that new employee gets off work, the first thing a friend or family member will ask is: *So, how'd it go? How do you like your new job? How's your boss?*

This is why it's a must to visit with your new employee for 10 or 15 minutes before they leave so you can get their feedback and reinforce their decision to join your team. Use this time to reinforce the positives and defuse any negatives.

## End of First Day Guidelines:

1. If the new employee's first day went great, this discussion will be easy. If things did not go the way they were supposed to, this will be a crucial discussion because it is your opportunity to handle any damaging impressions or problems before they fester. It's probably your only chance to turn a negative experience into a positive one.

2. We know from customer service research that when you solve someone's problem and turn it into a positive experience, that person not only becomes "satisfied," but they will actually become an "apostle" for your organization. So, just as you would never let a frustrated customer leave, never let a new hire go home upset or frustrated on their first day.

If the employee reports any problems or concerns during this meeting, there is a simple three-step formula called "Feel, Felt, Found" that's widely used in Customer Service circles and is just as effective with dissatisfied employees as well.

After the person voices their complaint:

- Feel: *I understand why you feel that way.*

- Felt: *I would have felt the same if that happened to me* or *I felt the same when something like that happened to me.*

- Found: *Here's what I've found our choices are to correct the situation:* list two or three ways to correct the situation and ask: *Which would you prefer?*

Remember, when friends or family ask your new hire how it went on the first day, the answer needs to be: *Great. Fantastic. I can't wait to go back tomorrow. I am going to love this job.*

## Meeting Agenda:

1. **Position the Person to Tell You the Truth:** *Hi, [person's name]. I just want to find out how your day went and what you think we could do to make everyone's first day on the job better.*

2. **Ask These Questions Before Someone Else Does:**

   - *How was your day?*

   - *How do you like your new job?*

   - *What do you think about the company so far?*

3. **Ask These Questions to Improve Your Process & Head Off Problems:**

   - *Did you have all the tools, information, and training you needed to feel comfortable here today?*

   - *Do you have any questions or concerns?*

   - *How would you rate your day on a scale of 1 – 10? Why did you give it that rating?*

   - *What did we do right? What could we have done to make it [even] better? Is there anything else we could do better?* (Probe.) *What is the best thing that happened to you today?*

   - *What was the most frustrating, boring, or confusing thing about today?* If the new hire responds, say you're glad he/she shared the information, use the Feel, Felt, Found formula, ask if they have any ideas about how to improve things and tell them what you will do (changes you can make or sharing the feed-back with management, etc.).

4. **Close on a Positive Note:** Then, just as you'd thank a customer for coming in, reinforce your new hire's decision and close on some positives.

5. **Keep Your Finger on the Pulse: If the first day went poorly, check back with the new hire frequently. If it went great, keep the good vibes going. It would be best if you touch base for about five minutes two or three times between their second and fifth days on the job. Remember, you, your fellow employees, and your department, store, or company will be the topic of conversation in the new hire's world for at least the next week.**

6. To maximize the power of first impressions, have your boss or your boss's boss or the company president get in touch with your new hire during their first week to welcome him/her to the organization and ask how it's going. This simple gesture will blow them away.

Use the following checklist to keep the two first day meetings on track.[9]

---

[9] For a complimentary, full size copy of this checklist, visit *www.Humetrics.com*, Knowledge Center, Forms & Tools.

# First Day Checklist for New Employees

New
Employee: _____

Start Date
and Time: _____

❑ **PLANNING:**
Set start date and time, review employment papers, assign a buddy/mentor.

❑ **FIRST HOUR MEETING:**

    ❑ Meet and greet

    ❑ Share information and set the stage

    ❑ Correct poor first impressions

    ❑ Theft prevention

    ❑ Reassurance and day's agenda

    ❑ Invite questions

    ❑ Close on a positive note

❑ **TOUR OF FACILITY:**
With emphasis on safety equipment & introductions.

❑ **PROVIDE OR ORDER BADGE & UNIFORM**

❑ **EMPLOYEE HANDBOOK & REQUIRED PAPERWORK:**
I9, identification and authorization to work documentation, W4, etc.

❑ **ORIENTATION & TRAINING:**
Include an opportunity to be productive and positive reinforcement.

❑ **END OF FIRST DAY MEETING:**

    ❑ Position the new hire to tell you the truth

    ❑ Ask the questions you need to ask before someone else does

    ❑ Ask the questions you need to ask to improve your process and head off problems

    ❑ Close on a positive note and keep your finger on the pulse during the first week

## MAKE THE FIRST DAY THE BEST DAY THAT PERSON WILL EVER HAVE ON ANY NEW JOB EVER.

**Scary Story #3:**

# This Is the First Day of the Rest of My Life?

Then there's the story a first-time worker employed by a major grocery chain posted on Yahoo. She was excited for the opportunity and happy because she already had two friends who worked in the store. However, she wondered online if she'd made a mistake because her first day consisted of two hours of paperwork, three hours of customer service and safety videos, and one hour stocking shelves. The way this "orientation" was handled made her feel more like a burden than a welcome addition to the team, so she asked the online community if they thought she should hang in there or quit. The overwhelming advice was to quit.

# The 3<sup>rd</sup> First:
# End of the First Week

*Find a job you like and you add five days to every week.*
—*H. Jackson Brown, Jr.*

Now that you've worked so hard to make a terrific first day's impression and you've checked back with your new hire a few times during the week, the end of the first week is the time to capitalize on your investment.

It would be most effective if this 15 – 30 minute debriefing could be led by someone other than the direct supervisor (if that's you) because it's useful to have someone else collect feedback and the interest of another supervisor, manager, or "higher up" makes the new person feel just that much more important.

The goals of this meeting are to reinforce the person's decision to join the company, conduct market research, get "newcomer's feedback," and ask for job applicant referrals.

## Reinforce Their Decision to Join the Company

If someone new conducts this meeting, introduce yourself and share how you came to join the company, earn your position, and why you like your job and your employer. Regardless of who hosts the meeting, ask:

1. *How did the week go overall? How would you rate it on a scale of 1-10? Why did you give it that number? What could we do to make things better?* (If there are any complaints, use the Feel, Felt, Found formula to turn any negatives into positives.)

2. *Are you getting enough, too much or too little help overall? How's it going on the learning curve? How would you rate your progress on a scale of 1-10? How would you rate the way we teach? How could it be improved?*

3. *Has your new job lived up to your expectations? Did anything surprise you?*

4. *Do you feel prepared to perform all your job duties?* If not, *What area would you like more practice or training for?*

## Market Research

This is an opportune time to do some market research to understand why good employees apply so you can maximize the effectiveness of your recruiting campaigns.

5. *Why did you decide to apply for work with us? Why did you decide to take this job? If we wanted to hire more people like you, how do you think we could get them to apply?*

## Solicit Feedback

6. *Most of the ways we do things around here were the very best way to do them when we started and some things we've been doing the same way for years. Because you've only been with us a week now, you still have a newcomer's perspective. If you could change some part of your job,*

*what would it be and how would you do it differently? Is there anything else you would change?*

## Ask for Referrals & Close

Far too many employers miss this opportunity.

> 7. ***Can you recommend any former co-workers or friends who you'd like to see work here? Where do you think he/she will fit in? Why do you think that person would be a good match? Who is the best manager/supervisor you ever had? Why were they the best? Do you think they might want to work here?***

Then either:

    a. *Great. Would you like to ask him/her to apply or would you like me to give him/her a call?*

    b. *Great. We don't have any openings right now, but, when we do, I'll ask you the best way to get in touch with him/her.*

To close, ask for questions one last time and reiterate how glad everyone is he/she joined the team.

8. *Do you have any questions or concerns I can help with??*

9. **Either:** *I've heard/noticed you're doing a great job so far. We're glad to have you as part of our team.*
   **Or**: *I've heard/noticed that you have been doing a great job at _____, but _____ needs some work. How can I help you with this or what can you do to improve in this area?*

# End of First Week Checklist for New Employees

Employee: _____  Date : _____

☐ **REINFORCE THEIR DECISION TO JOIN THE COMPANY**

1. How did the week go overall? How would you rate it on a scale of 1-10? Why did you give it that number? What could we do to make things better?

2. Are you getting enough, too much or too little help overall? How's it going on the learning curve? How would you rate your progress on a scale of 1-10? How would you rate the way we teach? How could it be improved?

3. Has your new job lived up to your expectations? Did anything surprise you?

4. Do you feel prepared to perform all your job duties? If not, What area would you like more practice or training for?

☐ **MARKET RESEARCH**

5. Why did you decide to apply for work with us? Why did you decide to take this job? If we wanted to hire more people like you, how do you think we could get them to apply?

☐ **SOLICIT FEEDBACK**

6. Most of the ways we do things around here were the very best way to do them when we started and some things we've been doing the same way for years. Because you've only been with us a week now, you still have a newcomer's perspective. If you could change some part of your job, what would it be and how would you do it differently? Is there anything else you would change?

☐ **ASK FOR JOB APPLICANT REFERRALS**

7. Can you recommend any former co-workers or friends who you'd like to see work here with us? Where do you think he/she will fit in? Why do you think that person would be a good match? Who is the best manager/supervisor you ever worked for? Why were they the best? Do you think they might want to work here? Then either:

   a. Great. Would you like to ask him/her to apply or would you like me to give him/her a call?

   b. Great. We don't have any openings right now, but, when we do, I'll ask you the best way to get in touch with him/her.

☐ **CLOSE**

8. Do you have any questions or concerns I can help with?

9. Either: *I've heard/noticed that you're doing a great job so far. We're glad to have you as part of our team.*

   **Or:** *I've heard/noticed that you have been doing a great job at _____, and noticed that _____ needs some work. How can I help you with this or what can you do to improve in this area?*

---

**MAKE THE FIRST WEEK THE BEST WEEK THAT PERSON WILL EVER HAVE ON ANY NEW JOB.**

**Scary Story #4:**

# The Most Expensive Person
# You'll Ever Hire Is the One You Have to Fire

Now, let's take a look at the other side of the coin... the *Employee from Hell.*

I recently posted an item on my daily blog *(www.KleimanHR.com*) about the alarming rise in former employee vs. employer lawsuits. A reader quickly responded with a perfect case in point. Here it is, just as I received it.

*I once got stung with a lawsuit by a chronic employer-suer, who I was in too much of a rush to hire. He seemed just perfect and his references (who it turned out were terrified to say anything bad) said he walked on water. So I had a lying, drug-using near psychotic, who lied like crazy in court about things that never happened, and even though I had witnesses, he won on one of his ridiculous claims in court after my life (and the lives of others) were turned upside down for months by depositions, hearings, etc. So I got religion on this one, believe me. I didn't dare post all the details today because I figured the nut might read it and find a way to sue me again. Keep spreading the message! It's important. (You need to hire tough and don't believe everything you hear).*

## The moral of the story: Learn to fire fast!

# The 4<sup>th</sup> First:
# Presenting the First Paycheck

*Never confuse the size of a person's paycheck with the importance of their job.* –Mel Kleiman

When you are lucky enough to be a person's very first employer, you have an obligation to set the standards and expectations that will guide the rest of their working years. If you are not the first employer, it's an opportunity to reset those standards if need be.

In most cases, this conversation is about giving information rather than getting it and tying this conversation to the presentation of the first paycheck underlines the importance of your feedback and strengthens the employee's relationship with you, the job, and the company.

More than ninety-five percent of the time, this will be one of the easiest conversations you'll have with new hires because most will try their best to be everything you expect. Even if they aren't "perfect," you will still have a good feel for whether or not they have the attitude and capacities needed to be a successful member of your team and it will be a positive conversation.

This conversation may be a bit more difficult with the less than five percent who just don't seem to be working out, but it is by far easier to have this talk after two weeks than after two months or two years.

By the time you are ready to present the first paycheck,[10] you should have a good sense of whether the person is either: (1) a real asset, (2) has the potential to become an asset, or (3) is already a liability.

**In the case where the new hire is clearly a liability, it is vitally important for you to learn to fire fast because an unhappy, unproductive employee who chose the wrong job or employer is detrimental to customer retention, staff morale, and your sanity.**

Think of this situation as a type of "catch & release" program. When there is not a good fit, it is a kindness to this employee, yourself and your organization to free him or her up to move on. If you don't release the person at this point, you most likely will create the conditions that cause major migraines down the road. (The best time to fire an employee is always the first time you think you should.)

If this employee looks like a keeper, but is not quite there yet (performance is satisfactory or borderline), presenting the first paycheck creates the ideal circumstance for resetting expectations as well as offering more help and/or training.

---

[10] Because the first paycheck has the highest probability for errors, before you present it, take the time to ensure the person's name is spelled correctly and that the pay rate and withholding amounts are correct.

When the new hire is clearly an asset, this is the time to reinforce "good behavior" with positive feedback.

Some suggested scripts follow…

## The Asset

*Hi,* [person's name], *have a seat. I invited you here because I wanted the privilege of presenting you with your first paycheck in person. Congratulations* [while you hand it over]! *Go ahead and take a minute now to look your check over and let me know if you have any questions. Does everything look right?* [If yes, *Great.* If no, explain and/or have it corrected.]

*From everything I've seen and heard, you're doing a great job and I just want to encourage you to keep it up. I noticed when you* [cite specific examples] *and that's the kind of thing that makes a big difference here.* [Go to the Performance Review discussion at the end of this chapter.]

## Borderline

*Hi,* [person's name], *have a seat. I invited you here because I wanted to present you with your first paycheck in person. Take a minute to look it over and let me know if you have any questions. Does everything look right?* [If yes, *Great.* If no, explain and/or have it corrected.]

*I think you're really trying hard, but I have a couple of concerns about your performance so far.* [List concerns with specific examples. Explain how these actions or oversights impact the entire organization.] *How best do you think we can get you on the right track?* [Then make your own suggestions (more training, different mentor, etc.). Gage the employee's eagerness to improve and, if there's a lack of enthusiasm or cooperation, suggest perhaps they'd like to move on if the job requirements don't suit them. If they are willing to try, agree to specific corrective measures.] *Okay, I can see you want to get it right and I expect a big improvement by the time your next paycheck comes due.* **[Go to the Performance Review discussion at the end of this chapter.]**

## The Liability

If you have decided to let this person go, before engaging in the following conversation, follow established company procedures.

**[Person's name]**, *have a seat. I invited you here because I wanted to present you with your paycheck in person. Take a minute to look it over and let me know if you have any questions. Does everything look right?* [If yes, *Great.* If not, explain and/or have it corrected.]

Use the following suggested talking points if appropriate, but be sure to follow your company's policies and procedures regarding terminations.

**[Person's name]**, *I do not know how you feel about your new job or the company, but I have to tell you I have serious concerns about your performance so far.* [List concerns with specific examples. Explain how these actions or oversights impact the entire organization.] *As you can see, this is not a good situation for you or for us and, in this situation, we've found the best thing to do is to go ahead and release you from our employment now so you can find a job that suits you better.*

Tell them what will happen next, how they will be paid for any unpaid time, what property they need to return, etc., and close with: *Thanks for all the time and effort you put in. I'm sorry it didn't work out.*

## Performance Review

If the person is an "asset" or "borderline," this is the best time to review "how they'll be graded." Although it may have been covered elsewhere already, so were a million other things, so go over it again so there is no question about what they are expected to do and how they will be evaluated from here on out.

*I also want to use this time to go over our Performance Review system so you'll know what to expect around 90 days after your start date. We want everyone to know how their work is evaluated and what the company and I really expect of you. I think the best way to do that is to give you the form we use so you will have a really clear picture of our expectations. Once you have been here about 90 days, I will complete this formal review and then you and I will go over it together. I think it's pretty self-explanatory and will give you a clear picture of what we look for. Take it with you and, if you have any questions after you've read it, just let me know.*

# First Paycheck Checklist

☑    Decide whether the employee is an asset, borderline, or a liability.

☑    Make sure the paycheck is correct before presenting it.

☑    Review the appropriate script and have the conversation.

☑    If you will keep this person on board, review the formal performance review system.

**Scary Story #5:**

# Promises, Promises

This one illustrates the costly fallout from management promises not kept.

*Six months ago, I left a lead position at a big box office supply store to accept a much lower paying position. Why did I do this? Because I was tired of being treated as if I didn't matter.*

*Within the first three months, I was thrilled to be promoted from Sales Associate to Lead. I was promised monthly bonuses, excellent benefits, raises, and much more. And through the whole thing, it was drilled into me how much the company believed in "Promoting from Within."*

*Throughout the year and nine months I held the lead position, I saw only two bonuses, benefits that took more out of my pocket than benefited me, and no raises after the initial bump for the lead position (although my duties tripled). No suggestions I made were ever taken, I was never considered for promotion, and I was barely even acknowledged by our District Manager or any of the higher-ups when they took time out of their schedules to actually make it to our store.*

*I keep in contact with my ex-co-workers, and have discovered that it has only gotten worse since I left. Our District Manager refused to promote our top Assistant Manager to Store Manager because she was a woman. In fact, they demoted her after a year and a half (telling her she "wasn't that good of an Assistant Manager anyway") and gave her position to a new Assistant Manager who has been there less than six months. The new store manager they brought in had never worked for the company (so much for promoting from within). So where did I go?*

*Starbucks. Another large corporation in a small town, but this one is run properly. In six months, I have gotten two raises, full benefits (for anyone who works 20+ hrs/week), stock options, and soon, a promotion. Best of all, I have regained my happiness and sanity. Those are the most important things of all.*

*And on a side note...the "top Assistant Manager" from the big box store starts training with me next week.*

# The 5th First:
# End of the First 30 Days

*Time is money. –Benjamin Franklin*

You have been asking the applicant some hard questions during the past month. Now it's time to ask yourself the hard questions about your on-boarding process and how the new employee is performing.

The fifth *First* is a stop loss strategy. Unlike a formal performance review,[11] the **Thirty Day On-Boarding Assessment** is as much about how you and your team have performed in bringing the new employee up to speed as it is about the employee's performance. The form that follows will paint a clear picture of how well you have done during on-boarding and how well the employee has adapted to your systems, procedures and culture. In just a few minutes, you will be able to tell whether you should keep doing what you have been doing or change your process and/or change employees. This step will save you, your team, and your organization untold time, money, and grief because:

1. The longer you keep doing what you've been doing that isn't working, the greater the chances you will experience disruptive turnover and personnel problems.

---

[11] Where the focus is on making sure the employee understands and accomplishes all duties and responsibilities as well as on setting goals and objectives.

2. The longer an underperformer stays, the more costly and difficult it becomes to let that person go.

3. The #1 reason the best people leave is because managers put up with under-performers and all the good people get tired of dealing with or covering for the slackers.

---

4. **Over 50 percent of accidents happen during the first year of employment and, in nearly every case, the person involved gave warning signs that they should have been let go long before the incident occurred.**

---

When you gave your new employee that first paycheck, you also had a discussion based on the fact that you thought of that person as either an asset, a liability, or borderline. The *Thirty Day On-Boarding Assessment* form that follows takes you through nine questions that will help you decide once again whether to continue investing in this new hire or to cut your losses and helps you evaluate and improve your on-boarding process. (Were orientation and training thorough and well-organized? Did someone frequently solicit feedback from the new employee? Were all the tools and materials necessary to get up to speed provided on time? Did management and co-workers make the new hire feel welcome?)

The 5 Firsts by Mel Kleiman, CSP

# Thirty Day On-Boarding Assessment

For a full size, complimentary copy of this form, visit *www.Humetrics.com*,
Knowledge Center, Hiring Forms & Tools

| Yes | No | Ask Yourself... |
|---|---|---|
| ❏ | ❏ | 1. Does this person live the Company's values? |
| ❏ | ❏ | 2. Has this person shown initiative and an ability to work without supervision? |
| ❏ | ❏ | 3. Would the team miss this person if he or she or he were gone? |
| ❏ | ❏ | 4. Have you experienced any problems with this person to-date? (Excuses, reasons they can't do what's needed, dependability issues, etc.) |
| ❏ | ❏ | 5. Has everything possible been done to help this person succeed? |
| ❏ | ❏ | 6. Have you made sure this person knows what it takes to be successful? (1$^{st}$ paycheck review, regular feedback, etc.) |
| ❏ | ❏ | 7. Is there something else you could or should be doing to get them to where they need to be? |

IF YOUR RESPONSE WAS "NO" TO 5, 6, OR 7 ABOVE, INITIATE REMEDIAL ACTION, THEN
REVIEW THIS FORM AND ANSWER #9 BELOW WHEN YOU FOLLOW UP.

| Yes | No | Ask Yourself... |
|---|---|---|
| ❏ | ❏ | 8. Should you continue to invest resources (time, money, training, mentoring, etc.) in this person? If yes, why? If no, why not? |
| ❏ | ❏ | 9. If this person is not working out, was something missed or overlooked in the hiring process? If yes, how will you ensure it doesn't happen again? |

Final action:  ❏ Continue to invest in this person.
❏ Allow this person to find another place to work.

# Don't Stop Now!

While *The 5 Firsts* capitalize on the lasting value of first impressions, there are plenty of other opportunities to reinforce the relationship the employee has with you, the job, and the company.

## The First Anniversary and More...

*People often say that recognition and motivation don't last. Well, neither do bathing and brushing your teeth. That's why you do them every day!* – Zig Zigler

Recognition and motivation are business school terms for the many ways managers can connect with their people to help them feel they belong and are valued members of the team. Why are these subjects important enough to be included in the business school curriculum at Harvard? Because one of the main reasons good and great people leave is because management spends more time dealing with the problems the average and below-average people create than they do mentoring, recognizing, and encouraging their best people (a.k.a. *the squeaky wheel syndrome*).

Unfortunately, in a wide ranging Gallup survey of American workers, more than 65 percent said they had received no recognition at work at all in the past year.

On the other hand, when 1,000 employees were asked if they knew the date they started working for their employer, 97 percent said, "Yes." (Many even remembered which day of the week it was.)

Add to this the fact that The National Customer Service Association reports over 67 percent of customers[12] say they would go someplace else to do business if they thought it would be more fun and you have a recipe for disaster. Here are the ingredients:

1. Most employers focus on correcting the negative rather than reinforcing the positive
2. Most workers value and take pride in their jobs
3. No one's having any fun

That's why an employee's anniversary is the perfect opportunity to:

1. Give much deserved, positive recognition
2. Capitalize on employee pride
3. Have a little fun at work

Acknowledging length-of-service anniversaries is one simple, yet effective, remedy for this. It improves employee retention and helps build stronger, more cohesive teams. While most employees remember their exact start date, most employers don't and the messages this lack of acknowledgement sends are:

1. No matter how many times we say, "Our people are our most important assets," we don't really mean it.

2. If length-of-service (tenure) is not acknowledged, how important could it be? The lack of recognition implies

---

[12] Don't forget that employees are just like customers and most of them would also go someplace else to work if they thought it would be more fun.

that employee turnover is expected
and acceptable.

This acknowledgement needn't be elaborate or expensive. It can be as simple as a congratulatory card, a note of appreciation, or acknowledging the employee on your signage. How about giving the choice of best shift for a week or a month, the best employee parking space for a month, or a "Get Out of Jail Free" card that lets them turn down one job they'd rather not do one time? If you want to give something inexpensive, how about movie tickets or a gift card? A sheetcake costs next to nothing and the bakery will put the employee's name on it free. If you can be more generous, how about a half- or full-day off with pay?

Of course, the more closely you can tailor the acknowledgement to the particular person's interests and preferences, the better. And, whenever possible, the acknowledgement should be made in front of the entire staff to capitalize on the team-building component. (If you have a lot of repeat customers, include them too. Bet they'd think of your organization even more favorably if you offered them a piece of sheetcake every now and then.)

If you're thinking you're far too busy to plan and administer this type of program, delegate the job to the best people-person on your staff. It'll be right up their alley and they'll find it tremendously rewarding. There is one caveat, however:

**If you're going to do it at all, it cannot be hit and miss where some employees are recognized and others overlooked. Create a failsafe way to track all birthdays and employment anniversaries and a system to double check your work.**[13]

In cases where you have more than one length-of-service anniversary in a month or quarter, have a drawing for, say, the best employee parking spot, and then give the others another perk.

Every year's successive anniversary should certainly be acknowledged as well and, more than this, you, as the manager, are encouraged to look for other reasons to recognize and connect with your people, to celebrate and have some fun.

How about a birthday party once a month for all employees born in that month? (If there isn't time for once a month celebrations, do birthdays and anniversaries together once a quarter. Or a party once a quarter to celebrate everything – marriages, babies, graduations, birthdays, etc.). Other reasons to celebrate can be the accomplishment of specific goals or project completion dates. Put it on your calendar to come up with a reason to celebrate as often as possible. Budget constraints? Have a potluck, a picnic, or a piñata party. And community volunteer work of any kind taken on by your

---

[13] Don't delete this information when you lose someone you wish you could have kept. Instead, go ahead and stay in touch with these people. Maybe the grass wasn't greener after all and they'd like to come back.

team and supported by you will reap tremendous dividends all around.

Here are few other firsts you can use to teach, recognize, motivate, or celebrate:
1. First major mistake
2. First real success
3. First formal review
4. First raise
5. First promotion

And, last but not least, if you want to keep your employees continuously engaged and motivated, here are some suggested questions to ask them as often as you can.[14]

- ☑ What should we START doing?
- ☑ What should we STOP doing?
- ☑ What should we KEEP doing?
- ☑ Why did you come to work here in the first place?
- ☑ Why do you STAY?
- ☑ What is your dream job?
- ☑ What can we do to make your job BETTER?
- ☑ When do you feel most appreciated for what you do?
- ☑ How do you like to be recognized?
- ☑ What are you overdue for?
- ☑ What prevents you from doing the best you can?

---

[14] Most managers never get answers to the questions suggested because they never ask them.

☑   What frustrates you the most about the job, the company, and my management style?

There you have it... **The 5 Firsts** that will put you on the road to lower employee turnover and increased profits.

If the only *First* you adopt is the decisive *First Hour* conversation, you'll still be miles ahead of your competition. If you have the discipline and focus to institute them all, before long you'll find yourself in the enviable position of being an *Employer of Choice* because you've created a personal, emotional connection between your employees, their jobs, and your company.

# APPENDIX

Full-sized, complimentary copies of all forms
may be downloaded from:
*http://www.Humetrics.com, Knowledge Center, Forms & Tools*

# First Day Checklist for New Employees

New Employee: _____    Start Date and Time: _____

❑ **PLANNING:**
Set start date and time, review employment papers, assign a buddy/mentor.

❑ **FIRST HOUR MEETING:**

    ❑ Meet and greet

    ❑ Share information and set the stage

    ❑ Correct poor first impressions

    ❑ Theft prevention

    ❑ Reassurance and day's agenda

    ❑ Invite questions

    ❑ Close on a positive note

❑ **TOUR OF FACILITY:**
With emphasis on safety equipment & introductions.

❑ **PROVIDE OR ORDER BADGE & UNIFORM**

❑ **EMPLOYEE HANDBOOK & REQUIRED PAPERWORK:**
I9, identification and authorization to work documentation, W4, etc.

❑ **ORIENTATION & TRAINING:**
Include an opportunity to be productive and positive reinforcement.

❑ **END OF FIRST DAY MEETING:**

    ❑ Position the new hire to tell you the truth

    ❑ Ask the questions you need to ask before someone else does

    ❑ Ask the questions you need to ask to improve your process and head off problems

    ❑ Close on a positive note and keep your finger on the pulse during the first week

## MAKE THE FIRST DAY THE BEST DAY THAT PERSON WILL EVER HAVE ON ANY NEW JOB EVER.

# End of First Week Checklist for New Employees

Employee: _____ Date : _____

☐ **REINFORCE THEIR DECISION TO JOIN THE COMPANY**

1.  How did the week go overall? How would you rate it on a scale of 1-10? Why did you give it that number? What could we do to make things better?

2.  Are you getting enough, too much or too little help overall? How's it going on the learning curve? How would you rate your progress on a scale of 1-10? How would you rate the way we teach? How could it be improved?

3.  Has your new job lived up to your expectations? Did anything surprise you?

4.  Do you feel prepared to perform all your job duties? If not, What area would you like more practice or training for?

☐ **MARKET RESEARCH**

5.  Why did you decide to apply for work with us? Why did you decide to take this job? If we wanted to hire more people like you, how do you think we could get them to apply?

☐ **SOLICIT FEEDBACK**

6.  Most of the ways we do things around here were the very best way to do them when we started and some things we've been doing the same way for years. Because you've only been with us a week now, you still have a newcomer's perspective. If you could change some part of your job, what would it be and how would you do it differently? Is there anything else you would change?

☐ **ASK FOR JOB APPLICANT REFERRALS**

7.  Can you recommend any former co-workers or friends who you'd like to see work here with us? Where do you think he/she will fit in? Why do you think that person would be a good match? Who is the best manager/supervisor you ever worked for? Why were they the best? Do you think they might want to work here? Then either:

    a.  Great. Would you like to ask him/her to apply or would you like me to give him/her a call?

    b.  Great. We don't have any openings right now, but, when we do, I'll ask you the best way to get in touch with him/her.

☐ **CLOSE**

8. Do you have any questions or concerns I can help with?

9. Either: *I've heard/noticed that you're doing a great job so far. We're glad to have you as part of our team.*

**Or:** *I've heard/noticed that you have been doing a great job at _____, and noticed that _____ needs some work. How can I help you with this or what can you do to improve in this area?*

**MAKE THE FIRST WEEK THE BEST WEEK THAT PERSON WILL EVER HAVE ON ANY NEW JOB.**

# First Paycheck Checklist

☑    Decide whether the employee is an asset, borderline, or a liability.

☑    Make sure the paycheck is correct before presenting it.

☑    Review the appropriate script and have the conversation.

☑    If you will keep this person on board, review the formal performance review system.

# Thirty Day On-Boarding Assessment

For a full size, complimentary copy of this form, visit *www.Humetrics.com*, Knowledge Center, Hiring Forms & Tools

| Yes | No | Ask Yourself... |
|-----|-----|-----------------|
| ❑ | ❑ | 1. Does this person live the Company's values? |
| ❑ | ❑ | 2. Has this person shown initiative and an ability to work without supervision? |
| ❑ | ❑ | 3. Would the team miss this person if he or she or he were gone? |
| ❑ | ❑ | 4. Have you experienced any problems with this person to-date? (Excuses, reasons they can't do what's needed, dependability issues, etc.) |
| ❑ | ❑ | 5. Has everything possible been done to help this person succeed? |
| ❑ | ❑ | 6. Have you made sure this person knows what it takes to be successful? ($1^{st}$ paycheck review, regular feedback, etc.) |
| ❑ | ❑ | 7. Is there something else you could or should be doing to get them to where they need to be? |
| | | IF YOUR RESPONSE WAS "NO" TO 5, 6, OR 7 ABOVE, INITIATE REMEDIAL ACTION, THEN REVIEW THIS FORM AND ANSWER #9 BELOW WHEN YOU FOLLOW UP. |
| ❑ | ❑ | 8. Should you continue to invest resources (time, money, training, mentoring, etc.) in this person? If yes, why? If no, why not? |
| ❑ | ❑ | 9. If this person is not working out, was something missed or overlooked in the hiring process? If yes, how will you ensure it doesn't happen again? |

## Final action:

❑ Continue to invest in this person.
❑ Allow this person to find another place to work.

# Order Form

Shouldn't all the managers and supervisors in your organization have the benefit of the ideas in this book?

Buy **25** get **1** free ■ **50** get **3** free ■ **100** get **7** free ■ **500** get **50** free. For larger quantities, please contact us.

| | | | | |
|---|---|---|---|---|
| The 5 Firsts | _____ copies | x $13.95 | = | $_____ |
| Free Copies of The 5 Firsts | _____ copies | x $ 0.00 | = | $___0.00___ |

**OTHER BOOKS BY MEL KLEIMAN, CSP**

| | | | | |
|---|---|---|---|---|
| Hire Tough, Manage Easy | _____ copies | x $17.95 | = | $_____ |
| 267 Hire Tough Proven Interview Questions | _____ copies | x $12.95 | = | $_____ |
| 100+ 1 Top Tips, Tools & Techniques to Attract & Recruit Top Talent | _____ copies | x $12.95 | = | $_____ |
| 180 Ways to Create a Magnetic Culture | _____ copies | x $12.95 | = | $_____ |
| So, You Got the Job, Now What? | _____ copies | x $9.95 | = | $_____ |
| | Product Total | | = | $_____ |
| | Shipping & Handling* | | = | $_____ |
| | Subtotal | | = | $_____ |
| | Sales Tax (Texas only: 8.25%) | | = | $_____ |
| | Total (U.S. dollars only) | | = | $_____ |

*For actual shipping & handling fees, please visit The Hiring Store @ www.humetrics.com

Name _____ Title_____

Organization _____

Shipping Address _____

City_____ State_____ Zip _____

Phone _____ Email _____

Charge your order: ❑ MasterCard  ❑ Visa  ❑ American Express

Credit Card Number _____ Exp. Date _____

❑ Check enclosed (payable to Humetrics)

❑ Please invoice (orders over $250 only) ❑ P.O. Number (required)

**PHONE: (713) 771-4401    VISIT: The Hiring Store @ www.Humetrics.com**